THE
FORSAKEN
ROOT

Trevtee

Copyright © 2024 Trevtee
All rights reserved
First Edition

NEWMAN SPRINGS PUBLISHING
320 Broad Street
Red Bank, NJ 07701

First originally published by Newman
Springs Publishing 2024

ISBN 979-8-89061-249-6 (Paperback)
ISBN 979-8-89061-250-2 (Digital)

Printed in the United States of America

For you—Evelina, Claire, Jerry, and Rita.

Contents

Introduction vii

1. Creation of Man 1
2. What Does It Take to Believe 12
3. Protection against the Devil 16
4. Is God Really as Great as They Say 19
5. The Conqueror 31
6. Blessings 34
7. Higher Order 37
8. Faith 41
9. Fear 44
10. Relationship with God 46
11. Spiritual Development 48
12. Race and Racism 51
13. Road to the Future 57
14. Fruits of the Holy Spirit 61
15. Concluding Comments 66

Introduction

I am a proud Caribbean American with a birthplace in the Republic of Trinidad and Tobago. I emigrated to the United States in the middle 1970s—a place where I spent most of my adult life and a place where I have lived for over forty-six years now. I consider the American experience a refreshing one as it allowed me to evolve into who I really am. Most helpful to me in this journey was the upbringing I received from my parents.

I am the third of four siblings, and from an early age my parents instilled in us that a belief in God would help to guide our lives, and they directed us in that path. But this effort was also a shared value by the community in which we were raised. As a young boy, when I attended elementary school, it was required by the school that all students should gather at the designated prayer area to pray before classes begin; additionally, I attended church both on Sunday mornings and evenings. And to add to those routines, my parents taught us the art of praying. Unhelpful to us, whenever we missed church on Sundays, it didn't mean we had more time to play; no, we had to assemble at a makeshift "prayer room" in our home and pray—a ritual I never enjoyed.

I got married in my early twenties, and after two decades of family and work life, I became settled. It was at that time I started paying attention to my thoughts, and those I considered to be interesting, I made notations of them. I noticed whenever I had plans to go somewhere and felt it would give me an opportunity to write, I would take a notebook. On those occasions, I wrote mostly about the surrounding areas in which I was present or about different areas of life. Writing became one of my hobbies, and after compiling books of notations over several years, I felt a compulsion that there was something that I needed to explore and express in writing but wasn't sure of what it was.

I became interested in literature; and after reading several books, including the Bible, surprisingly, I saw areas within it that corresponded with some of the thoughts I had noted. I continued to read and

THE FORSAKEN ROOT

became an avid reader of this great book. Then I realized that all of life—whether truths, good, bad, or evil—was revealed therein. It was because of that revelation, I became observant about the manner we Americans live and interact with each other, especially over the last several years (2015 to present). These were some of my observations:

- a nation at constant war with itself
- laws being enacted to prevent rightful outcomes
- increased police brutality against people of African descent
- heightened acts of criminal behavior stemming from religious bias and racism
- a threatened future for coming generations of young Americans

While those observations were playing around in my head, I was struck with a "spiritual awakening" when praying one morning. God spoke to me through the Holy Spirit and said, *"I want you to write a book about me. Tell people about me because they do not know enough about me. Do not worry about what to say. I will tell you what to put in and what to take out."* It was because of that experience, along with my observations, that I was inspired to write this book. Additionally, because of my belief in God, I trusted what he said he would do to help me write it.

I believe we as a nation have reached a plateau—this plateau of human recklessness—because many of us have forsaken our root to idolize something harmful. As long as this behavior continues, man will keep on destroying man.

First, to explain our root: We are rooted in something deep, very powerful, and beyond the estimation of value that supersedes the layers of our parents, family tree, cultural heritage, and ancestry. And if we bind ourselves to it, goodness will always prevail. We are rooted in God, and a way to discover this truth is to examine where it all started. God's "creation of man" will not only take us there but will show us the doorway to the many things he has freely given to us, including their importance to our lives. To make this point and also show the presence of God in everything, I selected several citations from some of the books of the Bible.

Note: The word *man* is used interchangeably but represents both man and woman or men and women accordingly.

THE FORSAKEN ROOT

The words "Lord" and "God" are used interchangeably but are one of the same. Lord is referred to as God, and God is referred to as Lord.

The words "his" and "it" are used interchangeably to refer to the devil.

Creation of Man

The scripture outlined in this paragraph is the first gift that God gave to man: *"God created man in his own image, in the image of God he created him; male and female, he created them" (Genesis 1:27)*. It is a gift that is worthy of pause to mentally absorb and understand its intrinsic value, but we must unwrap it.

The purpose for which man was created: *"When God made the earth and the heavens—and no shrub of the field had yet appeared on the earth and no plant of the field had yet sprung up, for God had not sent rain on the earth, and there was no man to work the ground, but streams came up from the earth and watered the whole surface of the ground—God formed the man from* the dust of the ground and breathed into his nostrils the breath of life, and the man became a living being" *(Genesis 2:4–7)*. That man was Adam.

Then the Lord God said, *"It is not good for the man to be alone; I will make a helper suitable for him,"* *so the Lord God caused the man to fall into a deep sleep, and while he was sleeping, he took one of the man's ribs and closed up the place with flesh. Then God made a woman from the rib he had taken out of the man, and he brought her to the man (Genesis 2:21–22). That woman was Eve. The man and his wife were both naked, and they felt no shame (Genesis 2:25).*

God blessed man and woman and said to them, *"Be fruitful and increase in number; fill the earth and subdue it. Rule over the fish of the sea and the birds of the air and over every living creature that moves on the ground" (Genesis 1:28).*

God's intention was to have a name for everything he formed out of the ground: *"He brought all the livestock, the birds of the air and all the beasts of the field to man to see what he would name them, and whatever man called each living creature, that was its name" (Gen 2:19–20)*. Through that same concept, man also gave names to man and groups of men.

After man was created in God's image, he clearly stated his expectations. He warned man, *"Watch*

THE FORSAKEN ROOT

yourselves very carefully, so that you do not become corrupt and make for yourselves an image" (Deuteronomy 4:15). *Image* in this case means anything one idolizes as their God that is not of the true God.

(i) Sin of man

The sin of man began with Adam and Eve through deception by a serpent *(Genesis 3:1–19)*. Of all the wild animals that God made, the serpent was craftier than any of them.

God had planted a garden in Eden, and there he put the man he had formed. The Lord God made all kinds of trees grow out of the ground—trees that were pleasing to the eye and good for food. In the middle of the garden were the tree of life and the tree of the knowledge of good and evil. God took the man and put him in the garden to work and maintain it, and he commanded the man, *"You are free to eat from any tree in the garden, but you must not eat from the tree of the knowledge of good and evil, for when you eat of it you will surely die." (Genesis 2:8–18).*

While in the garden of Eden, the serpent said to the woman, Eve, *"Did God really say, 'You must not eat from any tree in the garden'?"* The woman said to the serpent, *"We may eat fruit from the trees in the garden, but God did say, 'You must not eat fruit from the tree that is in the middle of the garden, and you must not touch it, or you will die.'"* The serpent responded, *"You will not surely die, for God knows that when you eat of it your eyes will be opened, and you will be like him, knowing good and evil" (Genesis 3:1–5).*

When the woman saw that the fruit of the tree was good for food and pleasing to the eye and also desirable for gaining wisdom, she took some and ate it. She also gave some to her husband, Adam, who was with her; and he ate them too. Then the eyes of both of them were opened, and they realized they were naked, so they sewed fig leaves together and made coverings for themselves *(Genesis 3:6–7).*

As God walked in the garden of Eden, Adam and Eve heard his footsteps, and they hid from him among the trees of the garden. But the Lord God called to Adam, *"Where are you" (Genesis 3:8–9)?* Adam answered, *"I heard you in the garden, and I was afraid because I was naked, so I hid."* And God said, *"Who told you that you were naked? Have you eaten from the tree that I commanded you not to eat from?"* Adam said, *"The woman (Eve) you put here with me— she gave me some fruit from the tree, and I ate it."* Then Eve said, *"The serpent deceived me, and I ate" (Genesis 3:10–13).*

THE FORSAKEN ROOT

God said to the serpent, *"Because you have done this, cursed are you above all the livestock and all the wild animals! You will crawl on your belly, and you will eat dust all the days of your life" (Genesis 3:14)*. To Eve he said, *"I will greatly increase your pains in childbearing; with pain you will give birth to children" (Genesis 3:16)*. To Adam, he said, *"Because you listened to your wife and ate from the tree about which I commanded you must not eat of it, 'Cursed is the ground because of you; through painful toil you will eat of it all the days of your life. By the sweat of your brow, you will eat your food until you return to the ground, since from it you were taken; for dust you are and to dust you will return'" (Genesis 3:17–19)*.

Obviously, Eve and Adam were disobedient to God's warning. Whenever God speaks to us through whatever medium used, he will expect obedience; and if we disobey, he will leave us to whatever choices we may make because he would already know the outcome of those choices.

At some time in our lives, some of us would have experienced a serpent; but if we haven't, it does not mean that serpents do not exist. They present themselves in different forms and find delight being in numerous places: *"A scoundrel and villain, who goes about with a corrupt mouth; who winks with his/her eye, signals with his/her feet and motions with his/her fingers; who plots evil with deceit in his/her heart—he/she always stirs up dissension" (Proverbs 6:12–14).*

(ii) Birth of Jesus

To know about God necessitates knowing about his Son, Jesus Christ, to understand the role Jesus plays in our lives. When we think about Jesus, we should consider two things: *authority* and *intercession*. Jesus is often referred to as Lord and Savior, Son of Man, Bread of Life, and Lamb of God.

The nature of Jesus is this: *"He is the image of the invisible God, and the first born over all creation. For him, all things were created—things in heaven and on earth, visible and invisible, whether thrones or powers or rulers or authorities; all things were created for him. He is before all things, and in him all things hold together. And he is the head of the body, the church; he is the beginning and the first born from among the dead, so that in everything he might have the supremacy. For God was pleased to have all his fullness dwell in him"* *(Colossians 1:15–19).*

Because of the authority God gave to Jesus, Jesus intercedes for God. When we make requests to

THE FORSAKEN ROOT

God, we can expect that those requests will be interceded by Jesus.

After Jesus received all authority from God, one of his Disciples, Thomas said to him, *"Lord, we don't know where you are going, so how can we know the way?"*

And Jesus answered, *"I am the way and the truth and the life. No one comes to the Father except through me. If you really knew me, you would know my Father as well. From now on, you do know him and have seen him"* (John 14:5–7).

I must share with you that about twelve years ago at a funeral, I heard a conversation between two persons, one of which said to the other, *"When you are making requests to God, you have to go through Jesus."* The other person responded, *"No, I do not go through Jesus. I go directly to God!"* Based on that response, it would mean that the responder is not conversant with the authority that God gave to Jesus or that the responder has a back channel or complimentary ticket to God.

Note: If anyone has an appointment to meet with a director of a large firm and at the appointed day and time he/she goes to the facility where the director is located, does he/she go to the floor of the director's office, open his/her door, pull a chair, and engage in conversations with the director? The answer is no! According to most business practices, there are protocols that are followed to coordinate visits by members of the public. A visitor will first be met by the facility's security and afterward by a secretary or manager working under the director. It is by the same premise we are interceded by Jesus.

Jesus's creation remarkably distinguishes itself from all other creations. Jesus's mother, Mary, who was a virgin, was pledged to be married to Joseph; but before they came together, she was found to be with child through the Holy Spirit: *"Because Joseph, a righteous man did not want to expose her to public disgrace, he had in mind to divorce her quietly. But after he had considered this, an angel of the Lord appeared to* Joseph and said, *do not be afraid to take Mary home as your wife because what is conceived in her is from the Holy Spirit. She will give birth to a son, and you are to give him the name Jesus, because he will save his people from their sins" (Matthew 1:18–21).* Joseph followed the command of the angel.

Jesus was baptized by John the Baptist, who was sent by God to prepare the way for the coming of Jesus. John was baptizing by water in the Jordan River, and all the people in Jerusalem went to him. He preached a baptism of repentance for the forgive-

THE FORSAKEN ROOT

ness of sins, but John's message to the people was *"After me, will come one more powerful than I whose sandals I am not worthy to stoop down and untie. I baptize you with water, but he will baptize you with the Holy Spirit" (Mark 1:7–8)*. John was referring to Jesus.

At twelve years old, Jesus amazed his teachers. He went into synagogues and began to preach and performed wonders, miracles, healed people, etc., which God did through him. Jesus was aware that his life would have to be sacrificed through death to redeem a sinful world (sins which began with Eve and Adam), that there would be a plot to betray and condemn him, that one of his disciples would be the one to betray him, and that disciple would be Judas.

Jesus was flogged, spat on, struck on the head with a staff, then led away to be crucified. In his final hour, Jesus was nailed to the cross. Above his head, was placed the written charge against him: *"This is Jesus, the King of the Jews" (Matthew 27:37)*. Jesus cried out in a loud voice, *"Eloi, Eloi, lama Sabathani,"* which means *"My God, my God, why have you forsaken me?" (Matthew 27:46)*. Then Jesus cried out again, *"Father into your hands, I commit my Spirit,"* then he breathed his last breath *(Luke 23:46)*. "*For God so loved the world that he gave his one and only*

Son, that whoever believes in him shall not perish but have eternal life" (John 3:16).

Jesus was resurrected on the third day. God raised him from the dead, freeing him from the agony of death, because it was impossible for death to keep its hold on him *(Acts 2:24)*. Then when Jesus met with his disciples, he said, *"All authority in heaven and on earth have been given to me, therefore go and make disciples of all nations baptizing them in the name of the Father and of the Son and of the Holy Spirit" (Matthew 28:16–19)*. After the Lord Jesus had spoken to his disciples, he was taken up into heaven, and he sat on the right hand of God *(Mark 16:19)*.

(iii) The experience of Jesus's suffering

Consider some of the experiences some of us may have already faced in our lives or what we may face at some future time—hardships, challenges, difficulties, sorrow, grief, pain, etc.—which may toss us around or even shake us up. In the case of Jesus, we can learn something from his crucifixion. In the midst of his pain and suffering, he held on to his faith that the sacrifice he was making should complete its course so the intended goal will be achieved.

THE FORSAKEN ROOT

Having "faith" does not mean a problem or situation will go away or get resolved, but the exercise of faith will allow us to persevere through obstacles. However, one cannot have faith without belief. Belief is the ingredient on which faith relies. Jesus's crucifixion, as brutal as it was, is a model for us to adopt to strengthen our spiritual muscles in times of hardship.

When we are faced with challenges, we should ask for God's guidance and wait for his supply. Hold to the concept that "darkness" does not last forever; it always is overtaken by "light." Pray and wait for the light of God to come into your spirit to lighten the challenge or propel you over the challenge. *"And when you pray, go into your room; close the door and pray to your Father, who is unseen; then your Father, who sees what is done in secret will reward you. For he knows what you need before you ask him" (Matthew 6:6).*

What Does It Take to Believe

There are many men, some referred to as atheist, who believe there is no God, yet when they are faced with life-threatening situations (danger, peril, distress) or even non-life-threatening but burdensome situations seemingly out of their controls, they call out to God: *"Oh my God!" "What happened here!" "I don't understand!" "How could this have happened!"* Then they put *hot sauce* on their emotions and spew out: *"Oooh… myyy… God!"* They call out God's name in vain; they claim him; then they question him. Isn't it amazing that some unbelievers would choose to disbelieve what they really believe in their hearts about God—that he exists, yet they keep login IDs and passwords

THE FORSAKEN ROOT

locked in secret places in their memories so that they will never forget how to contact him. They all use the same IDs and passwords: ID: *UNbelv#1*, and password: *OMG#2isme.*

Thank God for giving us Jesus to intercede on his behalf. I would imagine Jesus would check the list comprising "believers" and afterward confront the Unbelievers: *"I am the Lamb of God! Who are you? I did not see your name on my list! Since you have claimed God to be yours, do you possess a document of title to substantiate your claim or did you complete the acceptance form which I normally give to unbelievers? I am aware your answer is no! Nevertheless, I do not turn away, unbelievers. Here's a new form. Please complete and hand-deliver it to me, but only when you are on your knees, this way I will know your 'Yes' is your 'Yes.'"*

All it requires is common sense to know that there is a God and that he rules over everything, but we must believe in and trust our common sense. When we see sunlight, nightfall, or even clouds floating in the sky, we can ask ourselves: Can man create any of those elements? Our common sense will tell us no! Then who is the creator?

It is by the same exercise of common sense that many believe that God exists, but they have strayed from him to worship different gods to fulfill lifestyles according to what the gods offer them. There are others who believe God does not exist because he is not in the flesh.

The reason why God is not in flesh is that he is not like us; he is of spirit. Could you imagine if God were in the flesh and were subjected to the same things we are subjected to and God can be seen making groceries or at sporting events, even driving an expensive car, and living to an old age and dying? That would not have been a good thing, and I will tell you why: Who would protect us?

God protects our lives daily even from the same things that God created (e.g., sun, rain, snow, darkness, etc.). He commands those elements. And it is because of his omnipotence to place limits on everything he created, our lives receive his protection. On the other hand, if there were no controls to restrict the activity of his creations, death would occur daily by millions or even billions.

Take for example: If the snow had a mind of its own and says to the rain, "I am a little bored, so I am going to snow on earth for four consecutive weeks and ten feet high, so prevent your rain from showering during that time," then the rain becomes angry and notifies the sun of the snow's intention, then the sun calls out to the snow and says, "If you

THE FORSAKEN ROOT

release snow for four weeks and ten feet high, I will create sun that is of 150 degrees daily during the four weeks." In the meantime, darkness conspires with light to remain dark during normal daytime hours for those same four weeks. Who do you think will be affected? We will. This is why we need God's protection from both physical and spiritual harm.

Protection against the Devil

No one other than God is capable of protecting us from the onslaught of Satan, the devil, who is always busy trying to cause mischief. The devil continually seeks candidates to carry out its works, and we of our own might are not sufficient to ward off his schemes.

The devil also knows that it has no power over God. It is the opposite. Because of his jealousy and obsession with being equal to God, the devil tested Jesus. After Jesus fasted for forty days and forty nights, Jesus was hungry, and the devil came to Jesus and said, *"If you are the Son of God, tell these stones to become bread."* Jesus replied, *"It is written, man does not live on bread alone, but on every word that comes from the mouth of God" (Matthew 4:3–4).*

The devil then took Jesus to the holy city and had him stand on the highest point of the temple and said, *"If you are the Son of God, throw yourself down, for it is written, he will command his angels concerning you, and they will lift you up in their hands so that you will not strike your foot against a stone."* Jesus replied, *"It is also written: do not put the Lord your God to the test" (Matthew 4:5–7).*

In a further attempt, the devil took Jesus to a very high mountain and showed him all the kingdoms of the world and their splendor. He said to Jesus, *"All this I will give you if you will bow down and worship me."* Jesus replied, *"Away from me Satan! For it is written, worship the Lord your God and serve him only" (Matthew 4:8–11).* Then the devil left Jesus as he realized he could not corrupt him.

The encounters described between the devil and Jesus were note-worthy. In the third encounter, Jesus made a very profound response: *"Worship the Lord your God, and serve him only."* Jesus was reminding the devil that the Lord was his God too, so why stray from him to ask me (Jesus) to bow down to you (the devil)? This encounter also illustrated that "image" in itself, when manifested, can motivate corrupt actions as in the case of the devil's tempting. The devil wanted to be like God and therefore idolized an image of himself possessing the same power that God possesses.

I would go further to say: The devil has a likeness for big targets because of the power they hold, as in the case of Jesus. But whether big or small the target, the devil has one purpose and one purpose only, to *corrupt and destroy*. It has no allegiance to men other than to make them into disciples for the wrong reasons, then serve them with plates full of destruction. At no time, anyone will be able to say, "By the way, the devil died and left for me all this inheritance!" It will not happen. The devil will only go away if we increase the demand for God and help that demand to grow exponentially, then we may be able to say, "By the way, I heard the devil self-destructed due to lack of men to corrupt and carry out its works?" I therefore urge my brothers and sisters to stay close to God; embrace his goodness, and appreciate the benefits we receive daily because of his greatness.

Is God Really as Great as They Say

Let us examine some of the works of God and decide if he is really great. Let's take one which may seem trivial:

- What is the source that allows for "resemblance" to be inherited whereby a baby favors the features of either his/her mother, father, or other family members? The fact is that in pregnancy, women do not possess a kind of power that could dictate who their expected baby(s) should look like. If that were possible, then there might be plenty of Angelina Jolies, Halle Berrys, Derek Jeters, and Barack Obamas (people who are considered attractive or handsome).

Some of us even speak with the same tone of voice as well as take on the same physical shape as one of our parents. This element cannot and does not happen without the intervention of a higher power working through the womb of the mother. It is only God who can do such a thing.

Psalm 139:13–16 asserts, "*For you created my inmost being; you knit me together in my mother's womb. I praise you because I am fearfully and wonderfully made; your works are wonderful; I know that full well. My frame was not hidden from you when I was made in the secret place; when I was woven together in the depths of the earth, your eyes saw my unformed body. All the days ordained for me were written in your book before one of them came to be.*"

Though not trivial but certainly baffling, one of the great works of God is his mystifying structure of order. And the centerpiece of his order is his U-turns. Central to everything that God created or com-

THE FORSAKEN ROOT

mands, he has a U-turn embedded within it. In that way, everything is ordered to return right back to God. Again, it is only he that can do such a thing. Incredible!

Now let's look at some of God's works through his engagement with Job to see if we can glean his greatness as described in the Bible's book of Job (Chapters 1 through 42).

Job was rich; he had everything, but his sons used to take turns holding feasts in their homes and would invite their three sisters to eat and drink with them. They loved to party. Because of their behaviors and as a way of purifying them, Job used to sacrifice a burnt offering for each of them, thinking they would have sinned and cursed God in their hearts. But Job himself was a righteous man.

One day, angels came to present themselves to the Lord, and Satan came with them. The Lord said to Satan, *"Where have you come from?"* Satan replied, *"From roaming through the earth and going back and forth in it."*

TREVTEE

The Lord said to Satan, *"Have you considered my servant Job? There is no one on earth like him; he is blameless and upright, a man who fears God and shuns evil."* Satan replied, *"Does Job fear God for nothing? Have you not put a hedge around him and his household and everything he has? You have blessed the work of his hands so that his flocks and herds are spread throughout the land. But stretch out your hand and strike everything he has, and he will surely curse you to your face."* The Lord said to Satan, *"Very well, then, he is in your hands; but you must spare his life."*

Job had seven sons and three daughters, several thousand sheep and camels, five hundred yoke of oxen and donkeys, and had large numbers of servants—a rich man was he. The devil inflicted Job with painful sores from the soles of his feet to his head. Job lost everything in his possession, including his seven sons and three daughters who died when the house where they were partying collapsed. On hearing this, Job got up and tore his robe and shaved his head. He then fell to the ground in worship and said, *"Naked I came from my mother's*

THE FORSAKEN ROOT

womb, and naked I will depart. The Lord gave and the Lord has taken away; may the name of the Lord be praised."

Job's wife said to him, *"Are you still holding on to your integrity? Curse God and die!"* Then Job replied, *"You are talking like a foolish woman. Shall we accept good from God, and not trouble?"*

Job eventually became very annoyed with God. When his three friends— Eliphaz, Bildad, and Zophar—tried to comfort him, he cursed the day of his birth. He thought God gave light to those who were in misery, thought his misery was concealed in the heart and mind of God, and he insinuated that it pleased God to oppress him while smiling on the schemes of the wicked. He asked that God leave him alone.

Furthermore, Job went on to question God's judgment:

> • *"Why do the wicked live on, growing old and increasing in power; they see their children established*

around them, their offspring before their eyes."

- *"Their homes are safe and free from fear; the rod of God is not upon them.*
- *"They spend their years in prosperity and go down to the grave in peace; yet they say to God, 'Leave us alone! We have no desire to know your ways.'"*
- *"Who is the almighty that we should serve him? What would we gain by praying to him?"*

Then he said to God:

- *"My feet have closely followed your steps."*
- *"I have kept to your ways without turning aside."*
- *"I have not departed from the commands of your lips."*
- *"I have treasured the words of your mouth more than my daily bread."*

THE FORSAKEN ROOT

Job was making his case to God that he was innocent of any wrongdoing and that he should not have been made to suffer as he did—that God should have had mercy on him if he were a righteous God.

The Lord answers Job out of a storm, *"Who is this that darkens my counsel with words without knowledge? brace yourself like a man; I will question you, and you shall answer me."*

- *"Where were you when I laid the earth's foundation; tell me if you understand? Who marked off its dimensions? Surely you know who stretched a measuring line across it?"*
- *"On what were its footings set, or who laid its cornerstone?"*
- *"Have you comprehended the vast expanses of the earth? Tell me if you know this?"*
- *"What is the way to the abode of light, and where does darkness reside? Can you take them to their*

places? Do you know the path to their dwellings?"

- *"Have you ever given orders to the morning, or shown the dawn its place, that it might take the earth by the edges and shake the wicked out of it?"*
- *"What is the way to the place where lightning is dispersed, or the place where the east winds are scattered over the earth?"*
- *"Does the rain have a father? Who fathers the drops of dew?"*
- *"From whose womb comes the ice? Who gives birth to the frost from the heavens when the waters become hard as stone, when the surface of the deep is frozen?"*
- *"Do you know the laws of the heavens? Can you set up God's dominion over the earth?"*
- *"Who endowed the heart with wisdom or gave understanding to the mind?"*
- *"Who has the wisdom to count the clouds?"*

THE FORSAKEN ROOT

- *"Have the gates of death been shown to you?"*

I couldn't help but be overwhelmed in a state of awe as I read God's response to Job. What a stark reminder God made to Job about his works.

Then Job replied to the Lord:

- *"I know that you can do all things; no plans of yours can be thwarted."*
- *"You asked, 'Who is this that obscures my counsel without knowledge?'"*
- *"Surely, I spoke of things I did not understand, things too wonderful for me to know."*
- *"You said, 'Listen now, and I will speak; I will question you, and you shall answer me.'"*
- *"My ears had heard of you but now my eyes have seen you."*
- *"Therefore, I despise myself and repent in dust and ashes."*

TREVTEE

The Lord blessed the latter part of Job's life with more than he had before. His wife bore him more children (seven sons and three daughters). It was said, nowhere in all the land were women found to be as beautiful as Job's daughters.

In God's response to Job, he was not boasting but making Job aware of his commands over the universe. Who would God boast to anyway, and when would he finish boasting? No one can envision in their minds what God does anyone can do. He cannot be compared with anyone or anything as everything was created by him; therefore, he cannot be held to any standards. The Lord God wants us to boast about him: *"Let not the wise man boast of his wisdom, or the strong man boast of his strength, or the rich man boast of his riches, but let him who boasts boast about this: that he understands and knows me, that I am the Lord, who exercises kindness, justice and righteousness on earth, for in these I delight"* (Jeremiah 9:23–24).

When we proclaim to have a belief in God, he will find a way to test the integrity

THE FORSAKEN ROOT

of that belief as he did Job. As previously described, after Job lost all his possessions, including his children, he said:

(1) *"Naked I came from my mother's womb, and naked I will depart; the Lord gave and the Lord has taken away."* He was declaring that he came into the world with nothing and he would depart with nothing.

(2) *"May the name of the Lord be praised."* In retrospect, he was expressing that God is unique, so he was praising God in the form of a commendation.

Although Job's wife said to him, *"Are you still holding on to your integrity? Curse God and die,"* nothing discouraged Job's belief in God as he responded to her, *"You are talking like a foolish woman; shall we accept good from God, and not trouble?"*

Job's behavior was an example of not giving up under pain and suffering. When we endure hardships, God is treating us as

TREVTEE

sons: *"For what son is not disciplined by his father. If you are not disciplined, then you are an illegitimate child and not a true son"* *(Hebrews 12:7–8).*

The Conqueror

There was something indicative of ourselves that arose during the exchange between Job and God when Job questioned God's judgment: *"Why do the wicked live on, growing old and increasing in power; they see their children established around them, their offspring before their eyes." "The rod of God is not upon them." "They spend their years in prosperity and go down to the grave in peace."*

The phrases that were used by Job are synonymous with the expressions we vocalize when we observe or hear of men who carry out wicked and evil deeds. We fret. We say, "Why is God allowing their behaviors to continue?" "When would he bring them down?" "Is there really a God?" According to Psalm 37:1–2, God laughs at the wicked: *"Do not fret because of evil men or be envious of those who do wrong; for like the grass, they will soon wither like green plants; they will soon die away."*

Although, and to our dismay, God would sometimes let men with the behaviors described by Job continue for a lengthy period of time, we should rest assured that God has a variety of tools from which to corner and conquer them. They cannot and do not escape God. The Lord declares: *"Can anyone hide in secret places so that I cannot see him? Do not I fill heaven and earth"* (Jeremiah 23:24)?

God is a patient God, and he watches those who carry out wicked and evil deeds to see whether they will turn and seek him or rather live in an illusion of "foreverness." Many of them choose foreverness. Their behaviors demonstrate that they have no fear for God; therefore, they do not consider that their lives might be measured by their own misdeeds, that the claws of destruction may find delight in lying at their doorsteps, and that the doors to their death would expand widely. Make no mistake. God eventually strikes—entrapment, destruction, pain, suffering, death, or something else. None of these has a preference over the other. They wear the same uni-

THE FORSAKEN ROOT

form, and they mean the same thing to God. All are under his commands, and all are under his mercies.

But can lives having lived in the manner that Job described some men yield blessings? How would they? If seeds of lemons are planted into the ground, will they be able to bring forth grapes to tables on festive occasions? And God does not hand out meritorious awards to participants of evil or wickedness. It is the opposite; he punishes instead.

Blessings

Blessings can be considered vehicles that are workaholics. They are directed by God and work tirelessly on his behalf to deliver positive outcomes; thus, they show up in all types of situations and knock unexpectedly on many closed doors, all to fulfill needs and to grant favors where they are appropriated. But blessings can sometimes be mistaken for luck. There is a big difference between the two. Luck is multifaceted. It is associated with either positive or negative outcomes—the good, the bad, or the ugly. Therefore, there is no spiritual source that supports it, whereas blessings are designed to bring outcomes that are only of goodness, and they are generated by God.

THE FORSAKEN ROOT

Furthermore, God has the power to turn any type of situation into vehicles and, likewise, use people in the same manner for the purpose of disseminating his blessings. Unlike luck, it has no inherent power to dictate anything.

We often hear people say, "I am blessed." When we say we are blessed, it is understood that we are speaking about God's blessings because there is none other than God that truly blesses. If we consider a gift we received to be a blessing, it was not the giver of the gift that blessed us; it was God. He used the giver to accomplish the outcome. In turn, we should consider using a medium to bless others. It would translate to a "thank you" to God.

Some people also say, "My life is good as it is, so I do not need to know about God." A reason why their life is as good as they say (hopefully it is of goodness) is that they may be a recipient of God's blessing, not necessarily based on their own deeds, but God may have bestowed his blessing upon one of their family members (a mother, father, etc.) and it made its way through the pipeline to them. On the other hand, whatever God gives, he can also take away.

The Lord God knows who, how, and when to bless; conversely, he knows how to deal with those

35

TREVTEE

who indulge in evil: *"The Lord works out everything for his own ends—even the wicked for a day of disaster"* *(Proverbs 16:4).*

Higher Order

One of the reasons why it is important to know about God is that after forming a relationship with him, it can lead to a higher order of self, thereby enabling one to experience the following:

- Gain an effective formula for navigating through the vicissitudes of life no matter how burdensome they may seem so when storms attack and crash against your walls, you will be like a house built on a rock—immovable. On the other hand, when outcomes seem unfavorable to your desire(s) or expectation(s), you will realize the hand of God in those outcomes. God works according to his own time, not ours.

- Live in rhythm with the spirit, not the mind, as the mind can sap your energy and even run your life if you let it. The clock of the Holy Spirit never changes the timing of its beats; it ticks evenly and smoothly without interruption in tense situations or high-paced surroundings. If we align ourselves to the rhythm of the spirit, we will experience peace, calmness, and self-control.

- Learn to observe and safeguard your thoughts. Treat what you think as money, which has a spending value of 100 percent mental energy. Do not squander your mental energy on unproductive, destructive, or idle thoughts. They will harm you. Practice cleansing the mind with thoughts that are of a serene nature. A clean mind generates power!

- Release power into your confidence by acknowledging that God created us "in the image of him." The capacity that God gave us is much more than we fully understand, and it is for us to use wisely, bearing in mind that God did not place any restric-

THE FORSAKEN ROOT

tions on us for acting in the essence and spirit of him. So dig deep into yourself, love who you are, and seek to find what God gave you!

- Let whatever is in front of you become your teacher. Look at it or them through the lens of consciousness; in that realm, it will bring you into the present moment thus enabling you to see the value of the thing(s) you are looking at. It awaits a relationship with you. When we are in the present moment, the idle activity of the mind will dissipate, and the "now" will lead us into a place of oneness and total control of the entire body.

- Break the "worry" habit. Curse worry, and if it returns, curse it even more! Mentally, say to worry: *"I recognize you. You are a killer who has been killing people for many decades, and you are not coming into my house!"* Bring in the "big gun" (God) into your house, and shut the door behind him. Pray (e.g., use Psalm 23, the Shepherd's Psalm), and place all worries and concerns into the hands of God, but do not take them back. Believe he will guide you, and he will. *"Who of you by worrying can add a single hour to his life?*

TREVTEE

Since you cannot do this very thing, why do you worry about the rest?" (Luke 12:25–26).

There are other psalms that may prove helpful to your day (e.g., mornings [Psalms 3, 5, 95, and 96], evenings [Psalms 4, 91, 134, 139], *taken from the NIV Rainbow Study Bible*). We also have to grow in faith and learn to dispel thoughts of fear.

Faith

Faith is defined as *"being sure of what we hope for and certain of what we do not see. By faith we understand that the universe was formed at God's command, so that what is seen was not made out of what was visible" (Hebrews 11:1–3).*

"By faith, Abraham, when God tested him, offered his son, Isaac as a sacrifice. He, Abraham, who had received the promises from God was about to sacrifice his one and only son, even though God had said to him: 'It is through Isaac that your offspring will be reckoned.' Abraham reasoned that God could raise the dead, and figuratively speaking, he did receive Isaac back from death" (Hebrews 11:17–18).

To say "I have faith" is insufficient until faith is able to manifest itself in belief: *"Without faith, it is impossible to please God, because anyone who comes to him must believe that he exists, and that he rewards those who earnestly seek him" (Hebrews 11:6).* Belief is the pillar that faith stands on, and faith serves as a reminder that God is real.

Faith is a powerful instrument of the Holy Spirit, and *"God did not give us a Holy Spirit of timidity, but a Spirit of power" (2 Timothy 1:7).* It is a muscle that should be exercised for it to peak. It has two important components of the fruits of the Holy Spirit: patience and self-control. Patience generates "longanimity" in faith, and self-control "fortifies" faith to resist feelings of surrender.

Our faith should be trained as if it were a "marathon runner"—one that runs up hills, down hills, through valleys, in sun, and in rain. Faith does not know about the quenching of thirst and has no inclination when it will reach the finish line, but it knows it will get there. It must fix its eyes *not* on what is seen but on what is unseen: *"For what is seen is temporary, but what is unseen is eternal" (2 Corinthians 4:18).*

"Let us fix our eyes on Jesus, the author and perfecter of our faith, who for the joy set before him endured the cross, scorning its shame, and sat down at the right

THE FORSAKEN ROOT

hand of the throne of God. Consider him who endured such opposition from sinful men, so that you will not grow weary and lose heart" (Hebrews 12:2–3).

Fear

Fear is defined as *"an unpleasant emotion caused by the belief that someone or something is dangerous and is likely to cause pain, or a threat; a distressing emotion aroused by pending danger, evil, pain; the feeling or condition of being afraid, whether the threat is real or imagined."*

There are two areas of fear that are important to understand: (1) fear that is real and (2) fear that is self-manufactured. The fear that is real is associated with truth. Information about the thing feared is usually available. The likely outcome of this fear can be assessed. It is also a fear that helps to protect us from danger.

THE FORSAKEN ROOT

The fear we should mostly be aware of and manage carefully is the one that we self-manufacture—usually, "fear of the future." We manifest in events that we think will happen at a future time. But we must conquer this kind of fear by holding to the belief that a fear of something in the future is not a fact of something in the future. We ourselves energize this fear by fueling it with the power it seeks, and when we engage in this habit our fear strengthens and we are overtaken by it.

If we find ourselves holding on to fears about something that we feel may take place in the future, we should let it go and let God! The fact is no one can see the future or can they speak on anything that they already experienced at a future time, so we should detach ourselves from this ghost. Only God can accurately predict the future. Whatever will happen in the future, whenever it happens, it will *not* be based on a prediction by the mind.

Do not give fear of the future a seat at your table! It is a sibling of worry and stress, and it helps to destroy the body. A relationship with God will help to guide you on how to manage fear.

Relationship with God

The steps to forming a relationship with God are very simple. First, register with him, and invest in his comprehensive "whole life" plan. God does not require eloquence but humility. Speak to him as you would when speaking to a friend or family member (e.g., say to God, *"I accept Jesus Christ as my Lord and Savior, and I submit myself through him to form a relationship with you. I stretch my hand out to you as a confirmation of this desire. I ask that you teach me your voice so when I hear it, I will know it"*).

God will respond to you through the Holy Spirit *(referred to as the Spirit of God)* and will encourage you to have prayerful conversations with him. You

THE FORSAKEN ROOT

will realize the Holy Spirit is more active in your life as an agent of God; and it will serve to guide, warn, agree, or disagree with your intended actions. It will also inspire you to perform deeds in keeping with God's will.

As your relationship with God develops, start learning the language of God. Be aware, God is an indirect God and speaks through different mediums: a person, a thing, or a situation (they are all members of God's voice). If God were to give us everything directly, we would never self-actualize. How boring is that, and how boring life would be? None of us can attain spiritual development without having a relationship with God.

Spiritual Development

Because we live in extraordinary and troubling times, we have to protect and at the same time nourish the minds of the young; and because religion was taken out of the public school programs, it makes it difficult to do so. In the meantime, Catholic and other affiliated religious schools (CARS) have maintained their religious programs. Taking into consideration those two events, it will tell us this: students who attend CARS would be better positioned to gain an understanding of Christianity than students who attend public schools.

Even if students of public schools attend churches on a weekend, they will still not be on par

THE FORSAKEN ROOT

with students who attend CARS, possibly because some students of CARS may also attend churches on weekends. What does this scenario say about the present and future spiritual growth of the nation's youths? Are we going to allow this gap to expand uncontrollably without remediating the problem? If not, would our kids be able to display proper control of their behaviors? Would they be able to defuse conflicts between themselves and their peers?

Haven't we often learned through the news media or otherwise that students, having lacked the cognizance to temper their behaviors and work toward peaceful solutions when settling quarrels, leave and return to their schools with firearms and in some cases engage in deadly shootings of fellow students—furthermore, some destroying their own lives through self-inflicted gunshot wounds? A relationship with God can prevent such outcomes from occurring, mainly because it will set in motion better control of a person's intended actions if meant to be violent.

First, the void of religion in public schools ought to be filled with effective alternatives. This is achievable. And we—those who are concerned about the nation's kids—should have a stake in the effort. As a start, a concerted appeal should be made to local politicians, churches, ministers of the word, and teachers who have had training on the subject to deliver this item.

As an example, a "pilot program" in religion can be introduced to communities to test responses. The results may be helpful in directing the next steps to be taken. Overall, the objective should be to provide our young, including young mothers and fathers with the tools necessary to play prominent roles in the spiritual development of their kids.

It is also important that the young be groomed appropriately on the truths of race, racism, and the importance of establishing healthy relationships with their peers. We should teach them to love each other regardless of differences they may see in someone's physical appearance. The overall goal will be to nurture the young with virtues essential for their value systems, then they will be able to impart to their own kids what they would have gained from their parents.

Race and Racism

Race and *racism* are topics that many would rather not discuss because of their sensitive natures. They are unpopular for many reasons, including ignorance by some regarding the truths about themselves and others. However, race and racism are not circumvented by God's works.

Regarding race, I selected two ethnic groups as part of my study since they are identified by colors: white people (considered people of European ancestry) and black people (considered people of African ancestry). The language and or label used to identify these two groups plausibly has caused a myth that has impacted them in one way or another. Let's look at race:

(i) Race

According to the book of Genesis, God did not create a white man, nor did he create a black man. He created *man* and *woman*. It was man who decided to call a race "white" and another race "black," and based on the different ethnic groups, man gave them a name.

When people conceive a notion that they are white or that they are black and based on such notion that there is some humanistic value added to or taken away from them or that they are better or worse than others because of their skin tones or hair differences, it is pure ignorance when measured against truth.

The book of Genesis should remind us: *"The Lord God had formed out of the ground all the beast of the field and all the birds of the air. He brought them to the man to see what he would name them; and whatever the man called each living creature, that was its name. So the man gave names to all the livestock, the birds of the air and all the beasts of the field" (Genesis 2:19–20)*. Likewise, man called people of European ancestry "white" and people of African ancestry "black."

THE FORSAKEN ROOT

Another notion conceived by many is that their race is superior to other races—absolutely ludicrous! Therefore, we should rid ourselves of this sense of ethnocentrism because it may have led to this fallacy being espoused. God did not create a "superior man" or a "superior woman," so how then could there be a superior race? It is astonishing that man has elevated his ego to think that he is superior to his own form of creation. We were made from dust, and tell me, since when is dust superior to dust? Implicitly, man forgets what God remembers about us: "*For he knows how we were formed, he remembers that we are dust; man's days are like grass, he flourishes like a flower of the field; the wind blows over it and it is gone, and its place remembers it no more*" (Psalm 103:14–16).

The anatomy of all men is similar; likewise, the anatomy of all women is similar. But as we are aware, the physical makeup of both genders is constructed with similarities that are identical in nature (e.g., two hands, two feet, two eyes, two ears, one nose, one mouth, one head, etc.); and no matter whatever man calls, God's creations cannot change their anatomy. Man cannot change it! This is why it is important for us to understand and appreciate the truth about ourselves so we may understand the truth about others.

We are human beings that are made equal to each other and should move away from the laws of man and adopt the laws of God so we will know that none of us is better than any of us, and who of us thinks the opposite will not escape the pathway each of us will one day travel to be shown the place God has chosen for us.

Blood brothers and blood sisters are what we are whether or not some want to believe it, and here is why: The red blood that arises from our bodies when our skins are pierced has a symbolic meaning. It is united with the blood that Jesus shed on the cross when he was crucified for our sins. Jesus was just like us, 100 percent in flesh and walked among men *(he was also 100 percent in spirit)*. It was by God's design that he made our blood red, not white, black, or any other color, so that we could be in accord with him through the blood of his Son, Jesus. I reiterate, we are related to each other through the blood of Jesus Christ!

(ii) Racism

Racism is not genetic; we were not born with it. We are taught to be racist. Forms which cultivate racism are person-to-person and group teachings. Of

THE FORSAKEN ROOT

course, there are other forms that bring about the same result, one of them being "systemic racism," a venture which is deliberately designed to infiltrate different sectors of societies with intended targets.

Importantly, we should reserve our judgment about racists and not think that all are bad people. They do good deeds too. They should be considered persons who were misled by their teachers about the truths regarding the subject of race, and those same teachers were also misled by their teachers. We should forgive them: *"If you forgive men when they sin against you, your heavenly Father will also forgive you. But if you do not forgive men their sins, your Father will not forgive your sins" (Matthew 6:14–15).*

Part of the global crises we face today is because of man's evil to inject racism into societies. Racism is of the devil, and it negatively impacts everyone in society. And have we ever noticed, if a *d* precedes the word *evil*, the word will convert to *devil*? Yes, *devil!*

The different methods used to enforce racism illustrate man's obsession and his hunger for power, money, and greed to gain economic and political advantages over other races, the results of which have caused, to name a few, resentment, hatred, unrest, inequality, discrimination, and indulgence of criminal behavior among men. Have we ever seen mourners weeping over a coffin filled with money, power, or greed? The answer is no! Man or woman will die and leave either of those obsessions, or either of those obsessions will die and leave him/her or them!

America, as great a nation as it is, is deprived by racism from achieving peace. It constantly wrestles to find this food. And we can ask ourselves sincerely: When was the last time America was at peace? The good of the nation is frequently threatened by its own. How long will it withstand this constant "overweight" resting on its shoulders? *"Any kingdom divided among itself will be ruined, and a house divided against itself will fall" (Luke 11:17).* It is reasonable to say "national unity" is usually found through sports or tragedies, and when those two events have either concluded or eased, racism resurfaces back to its place. Then where do we go from there?

Road to the Future

The road to a better future can and may evade us if we do not take the opportunity to know our root. First, we should know our tree of life, and it will direct us to our root.

Our tree of life consists of four essential parts: the root, the trunk, the branches, and the fruit. God is the root, Jesus is the trunk, the parents/guardians (including family tree, cultural heritage, and ancestry) are the branches, and we are the fruits. This configuration by way of its tiers should make us aware of the depth in which God placed us into his root. It was to sustain us in a way that leaves no room for evil forces to enter and corrupt our spirit if only we would acknowledge him as our God.

If we look at what is happening in America today or even in some parts of the world, it will tell us that the serpent evolved. It wasn't satisfied with just being crafty after deceiving Eve and Adam. It wanted much more. Although God cursed it *(Genesis 3:14 refers)*, it saw an opening created by man's abandonment of God, and it moved right in and took occupancy in the hearts and minds of many. It corrupted their spirit, then darkened the light of their bodies.

The serpent is now a mighty dragon, and it gained many followers who made it their god. It is in all walks of our lives, even in "high places," including politics. We can learn something from the case being made by some lawmakers and citizens that there is a relationship between the usage of high-powered guns and the carrying out of mass shootings.

On one hand, there is a clamor to ban certain high-powered guns from being purchased by citizens; but on the other, an environment is created which has the likelihood to increase gun purchases by citizens. It can be argued that the legalization of open carry in some US states is an example of that environment. Who will win this tug-of-war? The dragon seems to know because whenever talks about sensible gun reform arise,

THE FORSAKEN ROOT

it wags its tail with a smile; its followers are well positioned to move those talks from the front of the line to the back. But are high-powered guns or any type of guns the cause of mass shootings? Let's find out.

There is no difference between a gun and a motor vehicle when it pertains to killing people. They both kill. But if we place a gun on a shelf and park a motor vehicle in a garage and no one activates their motors, they will remain where they were placed peacefully and harmlessly. However, if one decides to activate either the gun or the motor vehicle and create havoc, none of the two items would have motivated the user's action(s) and none should be blamed for the havoc. Sadly, it points to the mindset of the user. Then what is needed—a renewal of minds?

Renewal can come when we open-carry God in our hearts and minds. It will help the lamp of our bodies, which may have been darkened to spark into an illuminated light, then we will *see* our brothers and sisters from a lens of goodness and act from the mode of love because we will think not only of ourselves but also of them and all others. *Luke 11:34–35 asserts, "Your eye is the lamp of your body. When your eyes are good, your whole body also is full of light. But when they are bad, your body also is full of darkness. See to it then, that the light within you is not darkness."*

I will say vehemently: If we Americans acknowledge the root that anchors our tree of life and become emboldened by unity, love, and respect for each other regardless of class, race, or creed, America will be the greatest of the greater. Not only will it be known as "the beacon of hope" but it will be a beacon of inclusiveness for all its people; moreover, it may emerge to be a model for other nations around the world to adopt—yes, a model! This is possible because God gave us the means by which this kind of anew can be achieved, but the means must first manifest in the bloodstreams of all Americans. What are such means? What is this very thing?

See! God knew exactly what he was doing when he created us. He just did not say, "Rule over the beast of the field, the birds of the air, the fish of the sea, etc.," but he mapped out the course of our lives to be in an orderly fashion to lead us to him. Through Moses, he gave laws (*Ten Commandments*) to control man's behaviors; and among countless things, through the apostle Paul, he gave a template from which to establish a system of values essential for living peacefully and harmoniously among men (us). It is referred to as "fruits of the Holy Spirit" (or "fruits") *(Galatians 5:22–23)*. This is the means which should manifest in our bloodstreams.

Fruits of the Holy Spirit

Love

Love is patient, love is kind. It does not envy, does not boast; it is not proud. Love does not dishonor others. It is not self-seeking; it is not easily angered; it keeps no record of wrongs. Love does not delight in evil but rejoices with the truth.

Joy

Joy is deeper than mere happiness; it is rooted in God and comes from him. Since it comes from God, it is more serene and stable than worldly happiness, which is merely emotional and lasts only for a time.

Peace

Peace expresses the idea of wholeness, completeness, or tranquility in the soul that is unaffected by the outward circumstances or pressures. Jesus is described as the Prince of Peace who brings peace to the hearts of those who desire it.

Kindness

Kindness is doing something and not expecting anything in return. Kindness is acting for the good of people regardless of what they do. It demonstrates compassion, consideration, sympathy, and humanity.

Gentleness

Gentleness is defined as a disposition that is even-tempered, tranquil, balanced in spirit, unpretentious, and that has passions under control. Gentleness is not an indication of weakness but of power and strength under control.

THE FORSAKEN ROOT

Goodness

Goodness is the state or quality of being good and finding joy in being good. It is of moral excellence, the best of anything, and general character recognized in quality or conduct.

Faithfulness

It is being faithful in the transaction of business, the execution of commands, one who kept his plighted faith, being worthy of trust, and being reliable.

Patience

Patience, in some biblical translations, is "longsuffering" or "endurance." It describes the capacity to continue to bear up under difficult circumstances not with a passive complacency but with a hopeful fortitude that actively resists weariness and defeat.

Self-control

Self-control means being strong, having mastery of self, and being able to control one's thoughts and actions.

TREVTEE

Some of us may not be aware, but our behaviors, whether good, bad, or evil, fall within the parameters of the fruits. They are either (1) in keeping with the fruits or (2) deviate from them. Therefore, the fruits are "standards" by which we can measure our behaviors to ascertain which one of the two areas they favor.

I must admit, I was raised in a family of staunch believers in God; and though I was aware of the fruits singularly, I wasn't aware of their significance as a whole product. And I assume there are many who are just like me when I wasn't aware. But I have now gained an understanding that the fruits should be an integral part of everyone's personal values; thus, I realized I was not in accord with three of the fruits (peace, joy, and patience) but I am working to bring them to fruition.

I highlight the fruit of "love." In my humble opinion, it is the most powerful fruit since it was by God's love that he sacrificed his one and only Son for our sins. Consider Jesus, who was not only in flesh but in spirit too, his creation was superbly unique over all creations; but in spite of that, God sacrificed him. What an awesome display of love! Furthermore, there is no other love that is greater than the love of God! When we give love or feel a love that emanates

THE FORSAKEN ROOT

from "goodness," we are in step with God's love manifesting through our bodies.

This is the same love that fosters beautiful relationships from which generations of men and women who look just like all of us are born, some evolving to be geniuses in various fields (art, craft, science, medicine, technology, etc.) that build state-of-the-art innovations around the world. It is this same love that men die following their dreams, fulfilling their purposes, serving their countries on battlefields. It is this same love that warms the hearts of men and ushers in an understanding that prods them to form peace treaties among hostile nations to prevent or mitigate atrocities of war. Even babies, prior to speaking their first words, express this love through their first smiles to let their parents know, *"I am yours, and I love you."* But who is the architect of this beautiful and sacred tonic that helps to nourish and invigorate our bodies, that make us love it so much that when we feel it, we say, *"It feels soooo goood?"* The Lord God is he—from him, love, yes love!

Concluding Comments

As I conclude my writing of this Book, I will leave with you one of God's truth: because the Lord God is our creator, he is inescapable, and he knows us all; therefore "*none of us lives to himself alone; and none of us dies to himself alone. If we live, we live to the Lord; and if we die, we die to the Lord. So, whether we live or die we belong to the Lord" (Romans 14:7–8).* Then it is better to live and partake in good deeds and die honorably to the Lord so our bloodlines will be blessed, and blessed, and blessed than partake in the devil's evil and die disgracefully to the Lord where people may say, *"Thank God he or she is dead, but look at his or her bloodline. My gosh, they are just like him or her!"*

THE FORSAKEN ROOT

Do not forsake this precious root from which we were created as it provides the pathway for us to evolve into our greatest self. Treasure it, and sing a melodious song of praise and gratitude to this awesome creator, God, that he will say, "I am well pleased with this son or daughter."

Thank you for taking the time to read this book. I hope you gained enlightenment from its contents and can now impart the same to others. Personally, what I gained from writing the book was a feeling of "deep satisfaction" that I did exactly what God, in Spirit, requested of me on that morning when I was praying, *"I want you to write a book about me. Tell people about me because they do not know enough about me."* Additionally, the contents of the book gave me confirmation that God is the greatest of all times. Amen!

May God bless you and yours in all endeavors, keep you safe on the busy streets, grant you good health and happiness, and nourish you with the fruits. Love to you from me, Trevtee!

About the Author

Because of the industry that Trevtee was once employed for more than two and a half decades, it gave him a background in business writing. He was formally tutored in this area. However, in reference to the subject covered in this book, he had to use a different approach from what his background dictates in order to appeal to a wide range of readers. This is where his writing warranted being more creative and at the same time infectious.

Trevtee's writing depicts a marriage between two of his hobbies: writing across different topics and listening to different genres of music. He has a deep love for both art forms but has always been intrigued by the kinds of layouts and orchestrations that composers/arrangers achieve when arranging jazz and classical pieces. Trevtee has come to realize that there are parallels between the art of creative writing and the art of arranging music. He believes what helps to make the layouts of both art forms effective are the elements they use (e.g., rhythm, mood, harmony, argumentation, plot, transition, pitch, and orchestration). Trevtee's writing of this book includes most of these elements. Outside of the foregoing, his spiritual foundation has allowed him to speak truth to readers, which he does by playing a character in the book.

Printed in the USA
CPSIA information can be obtained
at www.ICGtesting.com
LVHW091229250624
783940LV00002B/274